D1090643

Gareth's Guide to Becoming a

WORLD-RENOWNED
CHEF

BY KATE MIKOLEY

Gareth Stevens
PUBLISHING

Please visit our website, www.garethstevens.com. For a free color catalog of all our high-quality books, call toll free 1-800-542-2595 or fax 1-877-542-2596.

Cataloging-in-Publication Data

Names: Mikoley, Kate.
Title: Gareth's guide to becoming a world-renowned chef / Kate Mikoley.
Description: New York : Gareth Stevens Publishing, 2019. | Series: Gareth guides to an extraordinary life | Includes glossary and index.
Identifiers: LCCN ISBN 9781538220498 (pbk.) | ISBN 9781538220474 (library bound) | ISBN 9781538220504 (6 pack)
Subjects: LCSH: Cooks–Juvenile literature. | Cooking–Vocational guidance–Juvenile literature.
Classification: LCC TX652.4 M57 2019 | DDC 641.5023–dc23

First Edition

Published in 2019 by
Gareth Stevens Publishing
111 East 14th Street, Suite 349
New York, NY 10003

Editor: Therese Shea

Photo credits: Cover, p. 1 Kzenon/Shutterstock.com; cover, pp. 1–32 (background texture) Thiti Saichua/Shutterstock.com; cover, pp. 1–32 (design elements) VDOVINA ELENA/Shutterstock.com; pp. 5, 6, 7, 15 wavebreakmedia/Shutterstock.com; p. 9 Lapina/Shutterstock.com; p. 11 violetblue/Shutterstock.com; p. 13 ANDER GILLENEA/ AFP/Getty Images; p. 14 grafvision/Shutterstock.com; p. 17 Wasant/Shutterstock.com; p. 19 Rawpixel.com/Shutterstock.com; p. 21 StockLite/Shutterstock.com; p. 23 Cheriss May/NurPhoto via Getty Images; p. 25 FOX via Getty Images; p. 26 Deb Lindsey For The Washington Post via Getty Images; p. 27 Pat Greenhouse/The Boston Globe via Getty Images; p. 29 Maskot/Getty Images.

Printed in the United States of America

CPSIA compliance information: Batch #CS18GS: For further information contact Gareth Stevens, New York, New York at 1-800-542-2595.

CONTENTS

WORDS IN THE GLOSSARY APPEAR IN **BOLD** TYPE THE FIRST TIME THEY ARE USED IN THE TEXT.

LEADERS IN THE KITCHEN

If you've been to a restaurant, chances are you've enjoyed the work of a chef. You may not have thought about it, but a lot of effort went into making your meal. Many people helped put it together, and the chef likely contributed a major amount.

When you think of a chef, what do you think they do? Do you think of them as people who just cook? If so, you'll be surprised to learn there's a lot more chefs have to do. They have many responsibilities, and, depending on the type of chef they are, these responsibilities might vary slightly. But no matter the type, all chefs are multitasking leaders! Are you ready for this extraordinary life?

53

percentage of US chefs and head cooks who worked in restaurants or other eating places in 2016

SPOTLIGHT!

KITCHENS IN RESTAURANTS CAN BE BUSY AND EVEN HECTIC AT TIMES. CHEFS HAVE TO BE ABLE TO HANDLE—AND BE IN CHARGE OF—A FAST-PACED **ENVIRONMENT**.

Kitchen Control

Most chefs work in restaurants, but many work in hotels or other places where food is made. Chefs oversee what goes on in these places. More specifically, they're in charge of what happens in the kitchen. They often **supervise** a team of cooks and other food preparation workers and keep everything in the kitchen operating smoothly. They need to make sure the kitchen is safe and equipped with needed supplies.

Good organization can help a busy kitchen operate smoothly.

Excellent leadership skills are a must for a great chef. As the people who manage daily food preparation, chefs often have to answer questions from other workers and solve problems that come up. For example, if the kitchen is almost out of an important ingredient, the chef is probably the one to find a solution. Other employees in a restaurant's kitchen may see chefs as role models.

Chefs are also usually in charge of hiring and training new food preparation workers for their kitchen. This means they have to interview and find the best candidates for a job. Then, after hiring them, they have to teach the new employee how their kitchen works and how to do their job well.

▶ SPOTLIGHT!
SOME CHEFS MAY DELEGATE RESPONSIBILITIES TO OTHER WORKERS. FOR EXAMPLE, THEY MAY ASK SOMEONE ELSE TO TRAIN A NEW EMPLOYEE.

Being a Good Boss

For the most part, the chef is the boss of the kitchen. Being in charge might sound fun, but being a good boss is tougher than you think. Sure, you get to tell people what to do, but if something is done incorrectly, you may be blamed—even if you didn't do it! It's important for chefs to be firm with their employees, but not mean. There's a difference between being the boss and being bossy!

Chefs may work closely with the other managers, such as the front-of-house manager. This is the person who oversees the dining room and the servers.

COOK OR CHEF?

You may be wondering what the difference is between a cook and a chef. Although these words are sometimes used to mean similar jobs, they're actually not the same! There are many different ranks, or levels, of cooks and chefs, but in general, a chef is higher up than a cook.

Chefs have usually been working in their field for longer than cooks, but not always. Most chefs started as cooks and worked their way up to being chefs. Many chefs have a **culinary** degree, which means they went to a special school to learn how to be a chef. They may have also trained under a chef who taught them what he or she knew. This is called an apprenticeship.

4,000

→ number of hours of training during a 2-year apprenticeship

➤ SPOTLIGHT!
SOME HIGH SCHOOLS OFFER SPECIAL PROGRAMS THAT TEACH CULINARY SKILLS TO STUDENTS WHO THINK THEY MIGHT WANT TO BECOME CHEFS!

Getting the Grade

One way to become a chef is through work experience. Another way is by going to a school or college. Many chefs get their training from a community college. Others go to 4-year schools with culinary programs. Some schools, called culinary arts schools, are mainly for teaching the kinds of skills chefs need to learn. These schools usually require that a student got good grades and graduated from high school.

Many places offer cooking classes for young people. Ask an adult to help you find some in your community.

9

CHAIN OF COMMAND

Every restaurant is different, but normally, the head chef is the person in charge. The head chef might also be called the executive chef or the chef de **cuisine**. They oversee everything that happens in the kitchen.

Right below the head chef is the sous chef. If the head chef isn't there, the sous chef is in command. Even when the head chef is there, the sous chef may supervise many of the other cooks and help prepare meals. Below the sous chef, there may also be station chefs or senior chefs who are in charge of certain parts, or stations, in the kitchen. Below these chefs are usually a number of cooks. Depending on the size of the restaurant, cooks may only work at one station.

> ## SPOTLIGHT!
> A CHEF WHO SPECIALIZES IN DESSERT IS CALLED A PASTRY CHEF, OR A PÂTISSIER.

146,500 → approximate number of jobs held by US chefs and head cooks in 2016

Find Your Station

Head chefs usually work in all parts of the kitchen, but other chefs or cooks might stay in one place. It takes a lot of different people to create a great meal in some restaurants! The part of the kitchen in which someone works is called their station. There are grilling stations, frying stations, vegetable stations, and dessert stations. Even a chef that works all over the kitchen probably has a station they **specialize** in.

TYPES OF CHEFS

> head chef

> sous chef

> saucier (sauce chef)

> poissonnier (fish chef)

> rôtisseur (roast chef)

> grillardin (grill chef)

> legumier (vegetable chef)

> garde manger (pantry/ cold-dish chef)

> pâtissier (pastry/ dessert chef)

Many of the words used for chefs come from the French language. For example, sous means "under" in French.

11

AN ART AND A SCIENCE

When you're helping your parents in the kitchen, you probably follow a recipe. Chefs get to create their own recipes. Heston Blumenthal is a world-famous chef from England. He's known for coming up with some wacky, yet wonderful, recipes. In England, meat pies are a popular meal. For one of his creations, Blumenthal served ice cream that looked just like meat in a piecrust. He also made candles, forks, and knives that could be eaten. He even created edible wallpaper!

You can think of cooking as an art form. You might use crayons or paint to create art, but chefs use food. Can you think of an unusual combination of food that might actually taste good? Chefs do this all the time!

SPOTLIGHT!

MATH IS IMPORTANT IN COOKING, TOO. CHEFS FIGURE OUT HOW MUCH OF A CERTAIN DISH THEY CAN MAKE WITH ONLY A CERTAIN AMOUNT OF AN INGREDIENT. THEY ALSO MULTIPLY MEASUREMENTS WHEN COOKING FOR A LARGE CROWD!

Get Cooking with Science

Science is an important part of cooking. When creating new recipes, it's essential for chefs to know how different ingredients react. For example, some foods **congeal** differently depending on what they're combined with. Ingredients can change **textures**, shapes, and colors, too. Science can help us learn which foods taste best together. Everyone has different tastes, but science can help us figure out what most people will like—and what they won't!

Blumenthal is known for using science in his recipes. He used liquid **nitrogen** to make the ice cream for his ice cream meat pies!

Coming up with recipes is an art form, but so is food presentation. Presentation is how the food looks on the plate. Have you ever been at a restaurant and your meal came out looking so nice you wanted to take a picture of it? Someone in the kitchen worked hard to make it look that way.

Food presentation is important to chefs because people are attracted to ordering meals that look nice. If you've ever seen a server in a restaurant walk by with someone else's plate and thought it looked good, you know how this works. Maybe you were attracted to the food itself, but chances are you were also interested because of its presentation.

→ SPOTLIGHT!
SOME CHEFS SAY FOOD LOOKS MORE APPEALING ON A WHITE PLATE. IT MAKES THE COLORS OF THE FOOD POP!

Looks Good, Tastes Good

In 2015, a study by an Oxford University professor showed that when food looks better, it tends to taste better, too. The foods used in the study included salad and steak, but were not especially fancy. Researchers learned that the people contributing to the study found foods to be more flavorful when they were presented nicely. The study also established that presenting the food a certain way made it seem more expensive.

A garnish is something extra meant to flavor or decorate food.

SAFETY IN THE KITCHEN

One of the most important parts of running a kitchen is making sure everything is **sanitary**. This includes the actual food, the people making it, and the tools used to prepare it. Unsanitary conditions can make food unsafe to eat. You don't want people getting ill from eating your food!

The workers in the kitchen need to stay safe, too. Making sure this happens is another part of the chef's job. Possible **hazards** to kitchen workers include falling on slippery floors, cuts from sharp tools, and burns from hot ovens or stoves. A good chef takes special precautions to prevent these things from happening, like making sure a spill is cleaned up right away so no one falls.

→ SPOTLIGHT!

A DEPARTMENT OF THE US GOVERNMENT CALLED THE OCCUPATIONAL SAFETY AND HEALTH ADMINISTRATION (OSHA) MAKES SURE EMPLOYERS KEEP THEIR WORKPLACES SAFE FOR EMPLOYEES.

Dressing Safe

At some jobs, workers can wear whatever they want, but this isn't the case when you work in a kitchen. For the workers' safety, there are dress codes. This usually includes shoes with special soles to avoid slipping, long-sleeved shirts to protect against burns, and some type of hat or hair covering. Long hair needs to be kept up to make sure it doesn't fall into food and also to make sure it doesn't catch on fire!

OSHA also offers advice on how to make sure kitchen hazards, such as this one, don't happen.

THE WORKDAY

If you want to have weekends and holidays off, being a chef isn't the job for you. Most jobs in the restaurant business require long hours. Chefs, cooks, and other people in the business may start early in the day and work late into the night. They often work on holidays and weekends, too.

Chefs spend the majority of the workday on their feet. This can make the work especially hard and tiring. Being a chef can be a lot of pressure, too. If you make a mistake, someone's going to taste it. So why do people do it? It's usually because they love what they do. If you want to be a chef, you have to really love the job!

> **SPOTLIGHT!**
> SOME CHEFS OWN A CATERING BUSINESS. THIS MEANS THEY PROVIDE FOOD FOR SPECIAL EVENTS, SUCH AS WEDDINGS OR BIRTHDAY PARTIES.

Run Your Own Business

Some chefs own restaurants. These chefs might get to choose their own hours, but their work involves even more challenges than just being a regular chef. That's because they have to manage all the other parts of owning a business, like making sure bills and employees get paid. However, they get to be their own boss and own a place where people love to gather and eat! Would you want to own a restaurant?

Some catering companies provide food for hundreds of people at a time, while others do smaller parties.

PERSONAL CHEFS

While most chefs work in restaurants, some are employed privately. They're called personal or private chefs. Personal chefs are responsible for making restaurant-perfect meals in someone's home. They may be hired to cook meals for one person or a whole family. People who hire personal chefs often entertain others regularly, so these chefs still have to be able to handle making food for lots of people.

When you're a personal chef, you may have to plan according to people's taste in food. Restaurant chefs often make foods of various cuisines, but a personal chef might have a few dishes they know the person or family they cook for like to have regularly. Still, it's important to mix it up!

> **SPOTLIGHT!**
> SOME PERSONAL CHEFS LIVE WITH THE PEOPLE THEY COOK FOR. THEY STILL GET TIME OFF, BUT MAY BE EXPECTED TO WORK ODD HOURS.

What's the Schedule?

Personal chefs work different hours. It depends on their employer's wants and needs. Some personal chefs spend the whole day working in their employer's home, making all the meals for the day, while others just go to the home a few times a week. They might prepare and package a bunch of meals at once for their employers to eat over a period of a few days or weeks.

When you're a personal chef, you need to know what your employer likes and doesn't like. You might also have to cook special meals if they have dietary concerns or health problems.

COOKING IN THE WHITE HOUSE

The White House executive chef is the person who runs the White House kitchen and prepares meals for presidents and their families. This chef is also responsible for planning and preparing meals for large events. In 2005, Cristeta Comerford became the first woman and first person of Asian descent to serve in the position.

Comerford moved to the United States from the Philippines when she was in her early 20s and started out working in a hotel kitchen. She later lived in Vienna, Austria, where she learned new styles of cooking. In 1995, she was hired to work in the White House. She worked as an assistant chef under the executive chef for 10 years before she was appointed to the position of executive chef in 2005.

→ SPOTLIGHT!

A STATE DINNER IS A FANCY EVENT WHEN A HEAD OF A GOVERNMENT FROM ANOTHER COUNTRY COMES TO VISIT THE WHITE HOUSE. THE WHITE HOUSE EXECUTIVE CHEF IS USUALLY IN CHARGE OF PLANNING THE MEALS FOR SUCH AN EVENT.

450 → approximate number of people Cristeta Comerford beat out to get the job of White House executive chef in 2005

The Fresher the Better

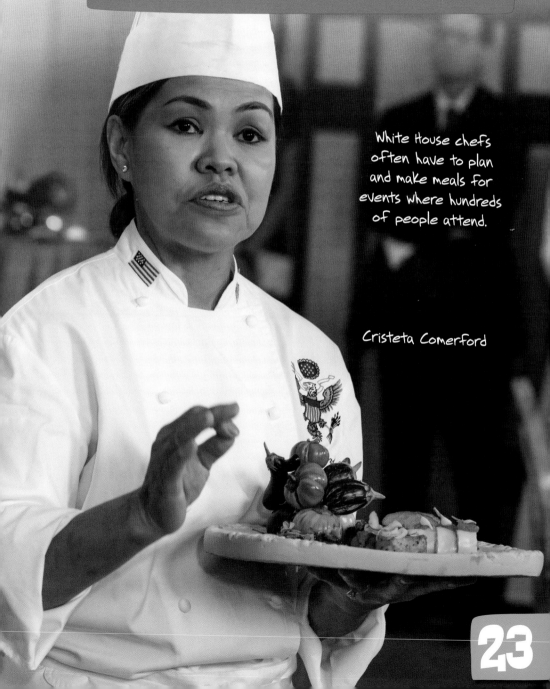

Over the years, the White House has been home to many vegetable gardens. During President Barack Obama's time in office, First Lady Michelle Obama promoted healthy eating and planted a large vegetable garden on the White House's South Lawn. Cristeta Comerford has said she used fresh ingredients from that garden, including vegetables and honey from beehives, in her cooking. Many chefs believe fresh ingredients are the key to delicious recipes.

White House chefs often have to plan and make meals for events where hundreds of people attend.

Cristeta Comerford

CHEFS ON TV

People love food! Some love it so much they even enjoy watching other people cook on television. If you turn on the TV and start flipping through channels, chances are it won't be too long before you get to a cooking show. Even Heston Blumenthal owes his rise to fame partly to television. Some chefs have their own shows, while others compete in contests on TV. Reality television cooking shows, such as *Top Chef* and *MasterChef Junior*, are some of the most popular today.

Cooking shows may be more popular than ever today, but they're nothing new. There were chefs on TV as early as the 1940s. Even before then, cooking programs were popular on the radio!

1946 → year the first cooking program aired on TV

24

> ### SPOTLIGHT!
> ON SOME REALITY COOKING SHOWS, SUCH AS *MASTERCHEF JUNIOR*, KIDS COMPETE TO MAKE THE BEST FOOD.

Food TV History

The first televised cooking program aired in 1946 and was just 10 minutes long. It was called *Cookery* and starred British chef Philip Harben. Just a few months later, a show called *I Love to Eat* aired in the United States. This show was 15 minutes long and starred chef James Beard who went on to influence many talented cooks. Today, there are TV channels that only air shows about food and cooking.

Sixth-grader Jasmine Stewart was MasterChef Junior's winner in 2017. She won $100,000!

When people think of early television chefs, many think of Julia Child. She wasn't the first, but she was one of the most successful. Child was born in California, but eventually moved to France. There, she learned all about French cuisine. Beginning in the 1960s, Child became well known by appearing and starring in cooking shows and writing cookbooks. Her cookbook *Mastering the Art of French Cooking* is very important in the culinary community. In fact, many people believe Child is responsible for bringing French cooking to the United States.

Child's show *The French Chef* first aired on a Boston television channel in 1962 and was shown across the country the following year. She died in 2004 but is still celebrated around the world today.

524

↘ number of recipes in Julia Child's *Mastering the Art of French Cooking*

→ SPOTLIGHT!

JULIA CHILD WON AN EMMY FOR HER SHOW *THE FRENCH CHEF* IN 1966. SHE WENT ON TO WIN TWO MORE EMMYS AND MANY OTHER AWARDS.

School Days

While living in France, Julia Child attended a cooking school called Le Cordon Bleu. She failed her first exam but didn't give up. She retook the test and graduated in 1951. Then, in 1952, Child and two other women, Simone Beck and Louisette Bertholle, opened their own cooking school! It was called L'Ecole des Trois Gourmandes, which means "The School of the Three Hearty Eaters." Lessons were held in Child's kitchen and cost $5.

In 2001, Julia Child gave the kitchen from her Massachusetts home to the Smithsonian Institution. It can be seen on display at the National Museum of American History.

GETTING STARTED

Most chefs learn how to cook through experience. They may start working in a lower position in a restaurant, such as a cook, server, or dishwasher. Eventually they may work their way up to sous chef and perhaps eventually head chef. But if you want to be a chef, you don't have to wait until you're old enough to work in a restaurant to get started!

If your parents cook at home, ask them if you can help. You might start with small tasks, like measuring the ingredients or washing the vegetables. They might not seem especially important, but these are tasks that chefs have to do, too. Every position in the kitchen is important—and even world-famous chefs have to set the table sometimes!

5 OR MORE

→ number of years of related work experience US chefs and head cooks usually have

> ### SPOTLIGHT!
> BAKERS ARE SORT OF LIKE CHEFS, BUT THEY GENERALLY FOLLOW RECIPES TO MAKE BREAD, CAKES, AND OTHER BAKED GOODS.

Starting From the Bottom

Like people in many fields, chefs often have to start from the bottom and work their way up. Many successful chefs started out chopping vegetables, wiping tables, or washing dishes. Thomas Keller is a famous chef and **restaurateur**, but his first job was as a dishwasher. It turned out to be an important part of his life. "The dishwashing station was next to where they cooked crabs, so sometimes I got to help the chefs," Keller said.

TIPS FOR BECOMING A WORLD-RENOWNED CHEF

> Help out in the kitchen at home.

> Find cooking classes in your community or at school.

> Invent your own recipes and try them out on your family.

> Get a job-any job-in a restaurant or other kind of kitchen and work your way up.

> Learn about many different kinds of cuisine.

> Attend a culinary program in college.

> Get an apprenticeship under a cook or chef.

GLOSSARY

congeal: to become thick or solid

cuisine: a cooking style

culinary: relating to cooking

environment: the conditions that surround and affect something

hazard: a source of danger

nitrogen: a colorless, odorless gas

restaurateur: a person who owns or manages a restaurant

sanitary: clean and free from things that might be harmful to one's health

specialize: to concentrate on a certain activity or subject

supervise: to watch over activities and make sure they're performed correctly

texture: how something feels when it's touched or chewed

FOR MORE INFORMATION

Books

Labrecque, Ellen. *Chef*. Ann Arbor, MI: Cherry Lake Publishing, 2017.

Meyer, Susan. *A Career as a Chef*. New York, NY: Rosen Publishing, 2013.

Siemens, Jared. *Chefs*. New York, NY: AV2 by Weigl, 2017.

Websites

Chefs and Head Cooks
www.bls.gov/ooh/food-preparation-and-serving/chefs-and-head-cooks.htm
Learn more about becoming a chef on the US Bureau of Labor Statistics website.

Recipes & Cooking
kidshealth.org/en/kids/recipes/#catrecipes
This site has tons of recipes so you can be a chef today!

INDEX